# PROFESSIONAL ADULTING
# <u>STARTERS GUIDE</u>

By: Maya J. Lewis

Copyright © 2017 by Maya J. Enterprises

All rights reserved.

Printed in the United States of America
ISBN – 978-1544751450
First Printing, 2017

Maya J. Enterprises
Atlanta, GA 30313

email: mlewis@professionaladulting.com
www.professionaladulting.com

---
LIFE STRATEGIZATION
---

# #PROFESSIONALADULTING

# TABLE OF CONTENTS

Step 1: Introduction
An Explanation Of Professional Adulting

Step 2: Transition In
Learn Strategies To Land Your First Job

Step 3: Learn The Environment
Understand The Professional Landscape From An Organizational View

Step 4: Participate At Your Own Risk
Career Mapping

Step 5: Define Your Brand
Professional Branding Strategy

Step 6: Kick Ass...Take Names
Performance & Appreciation

## PLEASE READ ALL INSTRUCTIONS IN THIS MANUAL CAREFULLY.

***Tools Needed:***
You
Interest
Desire to Succeed
Attitude (optional)

**NOTE:** *When considering the Professional Adulting process, please use your personality, tools and talents in accordance with how you were designed.*

## ADULTING

:to do grown up things and hold responsibilities.

## Step 1: Introduction
## An Explanation Of Professional Adulting

The urban dictionary defines adulting as a verb meaning to do grown up things and hold responsibilities. That immediately made me want to take a nap and try again tomorrow. "Grown-upping" or adulting is hard work. You are supposed to be present, dressed according to someone else's standards, responsible, studious...and a bunch of other things that again, make me want to take a nap and try again tomorrow. Professional Adulting is that hard work squared with a dollop of ice cream on top, where you are left to hope that the ice cream continues to make it worth it.

Lucky for me, I like ice cream and decided that not only did I want more than a dollop - I wanted to own the ice creamery. Not just because I like the impression I have as an overachiever, but because I realized that I wanted to help our generation have more than a dollop and have the confidence to admit when they wanted sorbet or a smoothie instead.

So I started my company, called Professional Adulting.

Professional Adulting as a verb is the display of mature and responsible behaviors in employment and entrepreneurial endeavors. Professional Adulting as a business is a lot of things but it is mainly my way of helping my generation change the world through their work.

It also provides me the opportunity to use my background in human resources to help organizations adapt to a Millennial driven workforce. But back to these mature and responsible behaviors in employment and entrepreneurial endeavors. Many of us have this silly notion that we can change the world...and I am a firm believer that we can. Honestly, we already have. In changing the world – some things have been completely transformed while others have started a slow transition. The workforce is on the slow transition train.

While I'd love to tell you that it should speed up this process and conform to our standards and expectations, I don't think it should. This slow transition is providing us time to figure out adulting without the world collapsing, giving us an opportunity to learn from experience without catastrophic events when we learn through our mistakes and allows us to learn more about the journey to the workforce of today, which can only help us in creating an awesome workforce in the future.

We can't fast forward to that future because, well...we can't. So we travel along this journey, one day at a time, one lesson at a time, one thought at a time. Hoping to tap into that thing inside of us that says that even if there was no dollop of ice cream I'd still do this. Professional Adulting is my thing. It has allowed me to help organizations and our generation along the journey and is allowing me to create this manual to help you along your adulting journey because our success as a generation is based on your success as an individual!

Enjoy!

**Step 2: Transition In**
**Learn Strategies To Land Your First Job**

On your mark. Get set. Graduate!!!

Now what? World domination? Domestic Engineering? Facebook trolling with early onset tantrums?

The transition from college to the "real world" can often be an exciting yet intense process. If you are part of the lucky few, you had a good career placement office and were encouraged to attend job fairs where you wowed the socks off scary people who referred to themselves as talent acquisition, making you wonder if the price for saying you'd show up in a suit again was worth it.

But maybe you didn't have career placement services. Maybe you couldn't make it to the job fair because of your workload and life demands. Maybe no one had socks on for you to wow. Maybe you still just aren't sure about what path to take. Hey…exhale. It is okay. Rome wasn't built in a day, and if it had been, it probably wouldn't still be standing. You don't have to have all the answers immediately. Really. You don't have to have any answers, if you know how to ask questions. But in case that didn't help, here are some things you can do to find a track and maybe even get on it.

1. Volunteer. Not only does it support your community and provide a need that might have otherwise remained in lack, volunteering is a great way to learn more about the things you like to do and are passionate about.

2. Build your professional network. This is how you find out about the job that isn't posted to LinkedIn or get the consideration for a position you didn't apply for.

3. Join and become engaged in professional organizations... related to your interest. It will expose you to different perspectives and maybe even help you find a profession you didn't know existed.

4. Spend quiet time alone...to think and maybe nap but mainly think. You want to grow and be in tune with your feelings and thoughts.

5. Become a Resolutionary...yes that is a word (see: bootylicious). Create or consider what challenges or limitations exist in your desired field and brainstorm solutions to/for them. You may stumble upon a niche or a global changing idea.

6. Have your resume reviewed...by someone other than the "adultier" adult you go to for help, unless your "adultier" adult is a professional resume reviewer or works in recruiting. This is to ensure that they aren't blinded by the awesome bias where they have special insight into your awesome and don't see how anyone else can't see it.

7. Envision and map out the future you want to have. Make a list of the jobs you want and the skills you need to build to get the longer term

ones. This will help you make job acceptance decisions.

8. Consider ways you can monetize your skillset independently. Who needs an employer anyway! Well, some people do, but if you can find a way to monetize your skillset successfully, you may be walking down a path called entrepreneurship.

9. Read. And social media articles do not count! Reading is fun but more importantly it uses da mental – get it…yes, I know it is a bad joke but you get the point. Keep your mind sharp, build your knowledge, increase your awareness and perspective. Your life will thank you later.

10. Accept that life is not fair. Get used to it even. Not in the way that there is exclusion for prejudicial things but in the way that says you won't have the ability to participate in every opportunity because of skill, ability or experience but there will also be awesome things that you get to participate in that will shape your future for the better.

11. Keep going. Again…it is hard but it doesn't get easier by giving up.

## Step 3: Learn The Environment
## Understand The Professional Landscape From An Organizational View

So here you are...looking for your first real job or better yet at your first real job or "sorta" real job or the place you ended up when you couldn't move back home and had to find a way to make it so you could eat and stream music on a regular basis.

In either case, the first thing I want to share (because others will be reluctant to share with you) is that you work at a business and that business has an objective and a goal. Some people in that business really value you and well, others don't know you exist and wouldn't be impacted if they never found out #theirloss. And that is okay because business is not all inherently good or bad. Your experience is largely based on your perspective and participation.

This is important to know because not understanding this could become a real ego bruiser.

Given your newness to this environment, you are in the introduction phase of the proverbial "Circle of Work," also what I call the Professional Life Cycle.

Exhibit 3.1

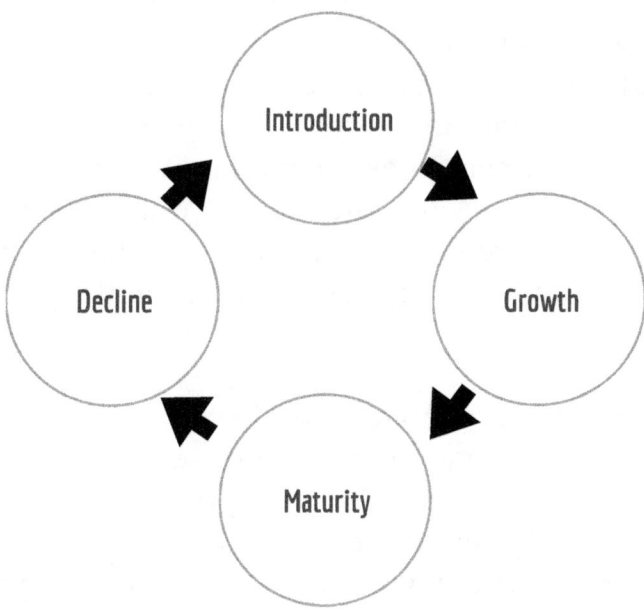

What this means is that you are new to the professional marketplace. In this stage, there is a need to create awareness and build experience. The focus is on heavy marketing and promotion activities (resume, interviews, networking, project learning) to increase your professional demand.

In your time ...not your co-worker, the guy down the hall or the friend who works at the other place – but your own time, you will grow and develop valuable skills and experience – increasing your demand. You will progress to the growth phase. Here your professional reputation will begin to speak for itself when you aren't around and you may experience opportunities abound. The work you do now will heavily determine the expediency and experiences available during the growth phase – so make it amazing...like you! Beware: The availability of increased exposure will be extremely exciting BUT don't lose sight of your ultimate goals (see chapter 4).

Traditionally, most people have been striving for the next phase, called the maturity phase. In this phase, people get comfy in their reputation, in their opportunities and competition. I know this seems like a foreign concept right now, and to be honest, it may be entering into the realm of archaic thinking given that technological advances and global workforces have taken away our ability to not stay current and competitive. Know this exists and when you spot it in the workforce, don't judge – help. Help that person learn the things that they don't know and listen as they teach you things that only time and consistency can teach.

And then there is the decline. Don't decline...reinvent your career. Always look for ways to stay relevant to you and your professional goals.

My point in sharing this is to help reduce the emotional and psychological conflict created as you experience technological advances that outpace the cultural adaptations, which may impact how SOME people value your work and opinion. I also want to help you understand one of the many dynamics at play in every office environment.

In spite and despite all of this, humble yourselves and take all information with a grain of salt. Some people will genuinely want to help you learn and understand. Others won't understand why you can't patiently wait your turn to have your voice heard. Don't settle but maintain a perspective of where you are. And remember that even if we are full speed ahead in life, going back to the future and past can provide you useful insight that could spark your creativity or give you the competitive edge against peers.

## Step 4: Participate At Your Own Risk
## Career Mapping

Once you've jumped in the water, there is no need in thinking you don't need to swim since it will still take effort and energy to just float. In non-metaphoric terms, become an active participant in your career, establish both short and long term goals, define your measures for success and then achieve them.

But be forewarned, participation won't always be easy. Don't try to throw the game just yet, grasshopper. Remember, this ish is hard...harder than hard. The great thing is though, if you actively participate, proactively plan and remain agile at the things that life throws, it can be extremely rewarding. Just know that all opportunity is not good opportunity and there is no such thing as failing...only learning forward.

View this as a journey where you stop and check your likes and snapchat messages. The other alternative would be solely looking at it as a means to a destination. While having a destination might be useful for guiding your path on the journey, only looking at it as a tool can make you seem like a tool. You lose perspective of opportunity/experiences and have diminished value for the unexpected which could be the piece to your puzzle of happily ever after.

Whatever you decide, here are some broad destinations that can help you assess opportunities along your professional adulting journey.

Exhibit 4.1

- Organization Participant – Use your skillset to help accomplish work
- Organization Leader – Use your varying skills to lead and achieve organizational goals
- Domain Expert – Leader in your segment of a field
- Breadth Leader – Aim for differing roles in field over time
- Field Expert – Collect expertise by looking at field from a 360 degree view

## Step 5: Define Your Brand
## Professional Branding Strategy

The world sees the person you introduce. That holds true for both personal and professional life. And if I'm being honest, #nojudgement zones only exist when people love you. The judging of the professional you will be based on the principles and approaches that guide your day to day decisions, actions, behaviors, and outcomes also known as your Professional Brand.

The good news is that creating your Professional Branding Strategy isn't a static equation or a finite answer. It is an evolving concept determined by who you are, what you know, what you are equipped to do and what you are motivated to achieve. Having a clearly understood Professional Branding Strategy will help you as you build the professional you and potentially give you competitive advantage over peers, which is helpful in performance reviews, promotional opportunities and even career advancement opportunities (read: new jobs).

I've adapted a business concept to provide a foundational frame of reference for consideration as you start to plan and build your Professional Brand Strategy.

Exhibit 5.1

| UNIQUENESS | SYNERGY | EFFICIENCY |
|---|---|---|
| You have a unique skill set or combination of skill sets that sets you apart in your field or profession. Your goal is to meet a need that organizations didn't know would benefit them. | You focus on creating relationships and bonds to accomplish goals and meet needs. You strive to find/develop win-win solutions to ensure the least amount of negative impact on the people and relationships. | You develop a keen ability to assess and identify process improvements that add value to the field or profession. Your goal is to minimize wasted time and energy. |
| You Create A Niche Environment For Your Work | You Strive To Maintain Close Professional Relationships And Large Networks | You Get The Most Done In The Least Amount Of Time... You Know, Efficiently |

Keep in mind, these are broad buckets and do not mean that there won't be times when you should allow the situation or environment to temporarily change your focus.

As with all strategy, there are risks and rewards associated with them all. Make sure you think about that and the alignment of your brand with your natural personality as you create your professional image blueprint. Feel free to create a compounded strategy or throw these out the window and develop your own.

## Step 6: Kick Ass...Take Names
## Performance and Appreciation

Remember how I said the No Judgement Zone doesn't exist...well not only does it not exist but in this wonderful world of Professional Adulting – you are judged constantly. Some organizations call it a performance review, some refer to it as an appraisal and others take a softer approach because they think we are sensitive and call it performance feedback. Just to be clear – it is all judgement. If done correctly and appropriately, this judgement is supposed to help you get and do better.

With that being said... time to kick ass! Be the best you that you can be. Given all the work you've done to get to this point, why half ass now? The media has tried to paint us as all getting participation trophies but we know that there are winners and losers. Nobody wants to be the loser! Just remember (while you are trying not to lose) to learn your team positions, manage your team expectations, and remember that appreciation and gratitude go a lot farther along than entitlement.

Maintain humility and appreciation in all that dopeness that is you because the celebratory party isn't as fun when it is just you and the deejay. But even beyond ensuring that there are lots of people to celebrate your success, remember that solid, productive and successful networks are built over time.

They are built in managers that you keep in touch with after realizing that it was time for you to move on to a new job, in the co-workers turned friends who help you stay connected in your industry and in the clients and customers you meet along the way. So take names and remember people...you never know who might be somebody someday.

**Note:** *Completion of this step may lead to increased attention and workload. Be sure to follow instructions from career mapping to guide decisions around opportunities that may present themselves.*

**IF YOU FOLLOWED THE PREVIOUS STEPS, YOU SHOULD BE ON YOUR WAY TO SUCCESSFULLY ADULTING – PROFESSIONALLY.**

## PROFESSIONAL ADULTING

:to display mature and responsible behaviors in entrepreneurial and employment endeavors.

---
LIFE STRATEGIZATION
# #PROFESSIONALADULTING
---

www.ingramcontent.com/pod-product-compliance
Lightning Source LLC
Chambersburg PA
CBHW061454180526
45170CB00004B/1707